Cloud Data Warehousing

Snowflake Special Edition

by Joe Kraynak

A Wiley Brand

Cloud Data Warehousing For Dummies®, Snowflake Special Edition

Published by
John Wiley & Sons, Inc.
111 River St.
Hoboken, NJ 07030-5774
www.wiley.com

For general information on our other products and services, or how to create a custom *For Dummies* book for your business or organization, please contact our Business Development Department in the U.S. at 877-409-4177, contact info@dummies.biz, or visit www.wiley.com/go/custompub. For information about licensing the *For Dummies* brand for products or services, contact BrandedRights&Licenses@Wiley.com.

ISBN 978-1-119-35192-4(pbk); ISBN 978-1-119-35190-0(ebk)

Manufactured in the United States of America

C10007090_122018

Publisher's Acknowledgments

Project Editor: Christina Guthrie

Acquisitions Editor: Steve Hayes

Editorial Manager: Rev Mengle

Business Development Representative: Karen Hattan

Production Editor: Antony Sami

Snowflake Review Team:
Vincent Morello, Jon Bock, Kent Graziano

Introduction

Arabic s an executive, manager, or analyst, you're well aware that knowledge is power and that data properly analyzed on a timely basis provides the insight necessary to make well-informed decisions and achieve a competitive advantage.

Today, companies have a much greater collection of more relevant data than ever before. This includes a diverse range of sources, internal and external, including data marts, cloud-based applications, and machine-generated data.

Unfortunately, the data warehouse architecture of the past strains under the burden of extremely large, diverse data sets. Analysts often wait 24 hours or more for data to flow into the data warehouse before it's available for analysis. They can wait even longer for complex queries to run on that data. In many cases, the storage and compute resources required to process and analyze that data are insufficient. This leads to systems hanging or crashing. To avoid this, users and workloads must be queued, which results in even longer delays.

To remain efficient and competitive, organizations must be able to harness the power of the vast amounts of data constantly being generated and conduct complex analysis on that data. Fortunately, advances in computer hardware, architecture, and software can help your organization meet this challenge and exceed your expectations.

About This Book

Welcome to *Cloud Data Warehousing For Dummies*, where you discover how your organization can tap the power of massive amounts of data conveniently and affordably to enhance efficiency and transform raw data into valuable business intel.

More data opens the door to more and bigger opportunities, which are almost always accompanied by equally big challenges. To take advantage of these big opportunities, you need to find and implement a data warehouse solution that can store and organize data in diverse formats, provide convenient access to it, and improve the speed at which you can analyze that data. And it must be done as cost-effectively as possible. This book shows you how.

Foolish Assumptions

We surmise that you grasp the concept of data warehousing and the challenges and opportunities it presents.

We also assume you're an analyst, database administrator, or other stakeholder or influencer in your organization, who wants a fundamental understanding of cloud data warehousing and how it can support the efforts and expertise of the people in your organization who need to access and analyze data. Or you may be a decision maker who needs the information and insight to choose the best data warehouse solution for your company.

Icons Used in This Book

Throughout this book you'll find the following icons that highlight tips, important points to remember, and more:

TIP

This icon guides you to faster, easier ways to perform a task or better ways to put cloud data warehousing to use in your organization.

REMEMBER

This icon highlights concepts worth remembering as you immerse yourself in the understanding and application of cloud data warehousing.

CASE STUDY

Throughout this book are case studies that reveal how various companies applied cloud data warehousing in real-world situations. They significantly improved the speed and performance of their data storage and analytics systems and saved money in the process.

Beyond the Book

If you like what you read in this book and want to know more, we invite you to visit www.snowflake.net, where you can find out more about the company and what they offer, obtain details about different plans and pricing, view webinars, access news releases, get the scoop on upcoming events, access documentation and other support, and get in touch with them — they'd love to hear from you!

Chapter **1**

Getting Up to Speed on Cloud Data Warehousing

I n one form or another, cloud computing and *software-as-a-service* (SaaS) have been around for decades. But cloud *data warehouse-as-a-service* (DWaaS) has only recently emerged as an alternative to conventional, on-premises data warehousing and similar types of solutions that have appeared in recent years. Why? Why now? What's changed? In this chapter, we answer these questions, and more.

We begin by defining what a data warehouse is and explore the evolution of data warehousing to understand how this technology has made its way to the cloud. Then we look at how organizations can benefit from cloud DWaaS and explain why more companies rely on cloud data warehousing to compete in today's data-driven economy.

What Is a Data Warehouse?

A *data warehouse* is a computer system dedicated to storing and analyzing data to reveal trends, patterns, and correlations that provide information and insight. Traditionally, organizations have used data warehouses to store and integrate data collected from their internal sources (usually transactional databases), including marketing, sales, production, and finance. The data warehouse emerged when companies realized that analyzing data directly from those internal systems competed with the day-to-day activities of business users such as data entry and operational reporting.

Over the years, data sources have expanded beyond internal business operations and external transactions. They now include exponentially greater volumes of data and more complex data from websites, mobile phones, online games, online banking apps, and even machines. Most recently, companies are capturing huge amounts of data from IoT (*Internet of things*)-enabled devices.

The Evolution of Data Warehousing

Historically, businesses collected data in well-defined, highly structured forms at a reasonably predictable rate and volume. Even as the speed of older technologies advanced, data access and usage were carefully controlled and limited to ensure acceptable performance for every user. This required businesses to be more tolerant of longer analytics cycles.

Times have changed (see Figure 1-1). Advances in technology mean companies can now make significant business decisions backed by large amounts of data. And it's not just the market leaders or mature companies. Smaller, nimble market entrants continue to transform well-established industries within months or just a couple of years. They're doing so with data to reveal opportunities and develop products and services that change how retail and business vendors engage their customers.

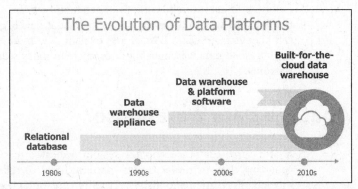

Illustration supplied by Snowflake.

FIGURE 1-1: Data warehousing has evolved over four decades.

Recognizing the limitations of conventional data warehousing

Conventional data warehouse solutions were not designed to handle the volume, variety, and complexity of today's data. And newer systems designed to address these shortcomings struggle to accommodate the data access and analysis that organizations now require. Today's challenges reveal:

>> Data sources are more numerous and varied, resulting in more diverse data structures that must co-exist in a single location to enable exhaustive and affordable analysis.

>> Traditional architectures inherently cause competition between users and data integration activities, making it difficult to simultaneously pipe new data into the data warehouse and provide users with adequate performance.

>> Scaling up a conventional data warehouse to meet today's increasing storage and workload demands, when possible, is expensive, painful, and slow.

>> The more recent, alternative data platforms are often complex, requiring specialized skills and lots of tuning and configuration. This struggle worsens when trying to handle the growing number and diversity of data sources, users, and queries.

But all is not lost! Like all great things, technology evolves. New ideas and new methods emerge to address the significant business problems of today and the aspirations of tomorrow.

Technology and design to the rescue!

The good news is that technology, and data warehousing *architecture* (the design and building blocks of the modern data warehouse), have evolved to address the demands of the data-driven economy with the following innovations:

>> **The cloud:** A key factor driving the evolution of the modern data warehouse is the cloud. This creates access to near-infinite, low-cost storage; improved scalability; the outsourcing of data warehousing management and security to the cloud vendor; and the potential to pay for only the storage and computing resources actually used.

>> **Massively parallel processing (MPP):** MPP emerged in the previous decade, which involves dividing a single computing operation to execute simultaneously across a large number of separate computer processors. This division of labor facilitates faster storage and analysis of data when software is built to capitalize on this approach.

>> **Columnar storage:** Traditionally, databases stored records in rows, similar to how a spreadsheet appears. For example, this could include all information about a customer or a retail transaction. Retrieving data the traditional way required the system to read the entire row to get one element. This is laborious and time-consuming. With columnar storage, each data element of a record is stored in a column. With this approach, a user can query just one data element, such as gym members who have paid their dues, without having to read everything else in that entire record, which may include each member's ID number, name, age, address, city, state, payment info, and so on. The approach can provide a much faster response to these kinds of analytic queries.

>> **Vectorized processing:** This form of data processing for *data analytics* (the science of examining data to draw conclusions) takes advantage of the recent and revolutionary computer chip designs. This approach delivers much faster performance versus older data warehouse solutions built decades ago for older, slower hardware technology.

>> **Solid state drives (SSDs):** Unlike hard disk drives (HDDs), SSDs store data on flash memory chips, which accelerates data storage, retrieval, and analysis. A solution that takes advantage of SSDs can deliver significantly better performance.

For more about advances in technology and other trends that drive the evolution of data warehousing, see Chapter 2.

Introducing the cloud data warehouse

Cloud data warehousing is a cost-effective way for companies to take advantage of the latest technology and architecture without the huge upfront cost to purchase, install, and configure the required hardware, software, and infrastructure. The various cloud data warehousing options are generally grouped into the following three categories:

>> **Traditional data warehouse software deployed on cloud infrastructure:** This option is very similar to a conventional data warehouse, as it reuses the original code base. So you still need IT expertise to build and manage the data warehouse. While you do not have to purchase and install the hardware and software, you may still have to do significant configuration and tuning, and perform operations such as regular backups.

>> **Traditional data warehouse hosted and managed in the cloud by a third party as a managed service:** With this option, the third party provider supplies the IT expertise, but you're still likely to experience many of the same limitations of a conventional data warehouse. The data warehouse is hosted on hardware installed in a data center managed by the vendor. This is similar to what the industry referred to as an ASP or application service provider. The customer still has to specify in advance how much disk space and compute resources (CPUs and memory) they expect to use.

>> **A true SaaS data warehouse:** With this option, often referred to as data-warehousing-as-a-service, (DWaaS), the vendor delivers a complete cloud data warehouse solution that includes all hardware and software and the IT and database administration (DBA) expertise required. Clients typically pay only for the storage and computing resources they use, when they use them. This option should scale up and down on demand.

For a more detailed comparison of cloud data warehousing solutions, turn to Chapter 5.

Why You Need a Cloud Data Warehouse

Any organization that depends on data to better serve their customers, streamline their operations, and lead their industry will benefit from a cloud data warehouse. Unlike massive, traditional data warehouses, the cloud means businesses big and small can size their data warehouse to meet their needs and their budget, and dynamically grow and contract their system as things change from day-to-day and year-to-year.

Here are a few areas where cutting-edge cloud data warehouse technology can significantly improve a company's operations:

>> **Customer experience:** Monitoring end-user behavior can help companies tailor products, services, and special offers to the needs and demands of individual consumers. With customer sentiment analysis, companies understand better what customers think by analyzing their social media postings, tweets, and other online messaging.

>> **Quality assurance:** Companies can also use the analysis of customer sentiment to monitor for early warning signs of customer service issues or product shortcomings and take action sooner than was previously possible when the only data source was call center complaint logs.

>> **Operational efficiency:** *Operational intelligence* (OI) consists of monitoring business processes and analyzing events to identify where a company can reduce costs, boost margins, streamline processes, respond to market forces more rapidly, and so on.

>> **Innovation:** Instead of only checking the rearview mirror to understand an industry's recent past, companies can use new sources of data to spot and capitalize on trends, thereby disrupting their industry before an unknown or unforeseen competitor does so first.

REMEMBER

Nearly all of a company's data is stored in a multitude of disparate databases. The key questions to ask are: How accessible is that data? How much will it cost to extract, store, and analyze all of your data? And, what will happen if you don't? This is where data warehousing comes into play.

Chapter **2**

Why the Modern Data Warehouse Emerged

Cloud data warehousing emerged from the convergence of three major trends — changes in data sources, volume and complexity; increased demand for data access and analytics; and technology improvements that significantly increased the efficiency of data storage, access, and analytics.

In this chapter, we describe these trends in greater detail for a clearer understanding and appreciation of cloud data warehousing. We also reveal how a data warehouse can take advantage of the benefits of cloud to address these trends.

Trends in Data: Volume, Complexity, and Usage

When we talk "data" in this book, we're talking petabytes. One petabyte is equal to about 500 billion pages of standard, printed text and can appear neatly typed in rows and columns in a database. Data also comes from people using websites and software applications on their phones and other mobile devices, or data produced by digital or mechanical devices.

In this section, we focus on changes in data, and data use, that have led to demand for cloud data warehousing.

The data tsunami

In the not-so-distant past, businesses generally managed data that was entered manually into the system by human beings. They may have also had data from external sources, such as customers, clients, and partners. The amount of data was relatively small and predictable, and stored, managed, and secured in a company's data center known as "on-premises".

Today, the business world is experiencing a data tsunami with data available from a variety of sources already mentioned in this book, and other sources too numerous and varied to list. The volume and complexity of this data can quickly overwhelm a conventional, on-premises data warehouse, and often cause data processing and analysis to hang, or even crash the system.

Adapting to the exponential increase of data requires a fresh perspective (see Figure 2-1). The conversation must shift from how big a company's data warehouse must be to whether it can scale cost-effectively, without friction, and on the order of magnitude necessary to handle massive volumes of data.

REMEMBER

The use cases that cloud data warehousing has sparked continue to emerge. For example, SaaS-born companies and big enterprises that use the cloud to store their data are monetizing (selling) that data. They package it as a service and sell it to other organizations keen to make better business decisions.

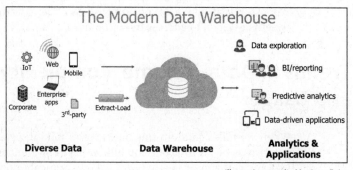

Illustration supplied by Snowflake.

FIGURE 2-1: The modern data warehouse enables all data for all users.

Data born in the cloud

The business world has experienced a rapid adoption of SaaS, including customer relationship management (CRM) software, business management (ERP) software suites, advertising buying platforms, and online marketing tools, just to name a few. Thanks to the cloud, new SaaS companies can set up shop with just the price of a laptop or two. These products can create huge amounts of valuable data stored in the cloud.

Demand for SaaS/cloud applications has also grown. Ease of deployment pales to what on-premises applications require to get up and running. In the past, a company may have operated only five to ten significant enterprise applications generating data. Now, it's normal for even midsize organizations to have hundreds or even thousands of applications, each with the potential of creating its own data silo — marketing data in one system, finance in another, product information in yet another — and none of them integrated for complete and optimum analysis.

With the majority of an organization's data now in the cloud, the natural place to integrate this data is also in the cloud. With cloud data warehousing, you can integrate cloud data in the cloud. You're no longer forced to pull it inside your data center, which is very expensive and time-consuming, and makes less sense as the amount of cloud-native data grows.

Machine-generated data

Machine-generated data is a key topic related to the *Internet of Things* (IoT). It's an endless collection of devices that communicate data via the Internet, including smart phones, thermostats, refrigerators, oil rigs, home security systems, smart meters, and much more. Data collected and analyzed from IoT devices can enhance products and processes, monitor equipment, and predict needed maintenance to avoid failure.

But a lot of machine-generated data has a poor signal-to-noise ratio. It contains valuable data but also a lot of "noise". Therefore, you often must store all of it to find the valuable bits. In addition, a growing share of this data originates outside your data center. This makes cloud, and its near-infinite scalability, the natural location to store and integrate this data.

Data exploration

Analyzing data starts with data exploration — identifying interesting and valuable connections and serving them up to data users in the form of reports and analytics. Although data exploration isn't a new concept, the growth in data volume makes it a more resource-intensive exercise.

Data exploration often involves large data sets. It's also often experimental in nature, which complicates the ROI assessment needed to support the significant upfront cost of deploying a traditional, on-premises data warehouse. In response, the cloud can enable a data warehouse to scale up and down as needed, and offers a pay-for-use model to avoid the challenge of whether or not to make an expensive, upfront commitment.

Data lakes

The growing need to have massive amounts of raw data in different formats, all in a single location, spawned the data lake. But companies quickly realized that transforming that data and extracting valuable insight was a cost-prohibitive, labor-intensive process to even attempt these efforts.

But the original interest in data lakes reveals that companies want to store all of their data in one location at a reasonable cost. With a modern data warehouse, the cloud supports the cost-effective methods to store and transform data with on-demand resources to minimize this resource-intensive process.

Trends in Reporting and Analytics

Data-driven decision-making is no longer relegated to the executive team or data scientists. It's now used to improve nearly every operational aspect of a company. But this increasing demand for data access and analytics across an organization can slow or crash a system as workloads compete for storage and computing resources from traditional data warehouses. Efficiency drops, requiring more time and money invested in additional infrastructure to maintain the system.

In this section, we identify some of the trends that are changing how people access and use data and how those trends drive the need for modern, built-for-the-cloud data warehouse solutions.

Elasticity to enable analytics

Here are a few scenarios where true, cloud-based elastic data warehousing can make it possible to do more with data:

>> As discussed earlier, data exploration has many benefits. But no one really knows in advance the computing resources needed to analyze huge data sets. This makes on-demand, elastic scalability ideal for this analysis.

>> Ad hoc data analysis answers a single, specific, business question, which emerges all the time. Dynamic elasticity provides the flexibility and adaptability to perform these queries without slowing down other workloads.

>> Event-driven analytics demand constant data. They incorporate new data to update reports and dashboards on a continual basis so senior managers can monitor the business in real time or close to it. Ingesting and processing streaming data requires an elastic data warehouse to handle variations and spikes in data flow.

Rapid iteration replacing exhaustive pre-planning

Entrepreneurs typically have two paths to follow when ensuring the marketability of a new idea: exhaustive preplanning or rapid iteration. The first option is a traditional, time-consuming process that involves thinking through an opportunity or a new product idea, kicking ideas back and forth, and hoping it creates consumer demand. Rapid iteration involves quickly testing the idea in the market to iterate over and over until a viable version of the product shows success. From there, the process begins again.

Rapid iteration has emerged as the more effective process to dismantling established competitors and altering how an entire industry does business. But it requires high-speed collection and analysis of a large amount of data to be successful. Advances in cloud data warehousing and analytics have made rapid iteration more practical.

Embedded analytics

For many companies, analytics operate as a separate and distinct business process. But a growing trend is to build analytics into business applications, which are increasingly built in the cloud. These applications handle significant variability in the number of users that query the applications and the number of queries (workloads) users run to analyze that data. The cloud facilitates data transfers from cloud-based applications to the organization's cloud data warehouse, where its scalability and elasticity can better support fluctuations in users and workloads.

MEETING INCREASED DEMAND FOR DATA ANALYTICS AT JANA

Jana provides free, unrestricted Internet access to more than 30 million smartphone users in more than 15 emerging markets. With its mCent Android app, Jana shifts the cost of mobile Internet from customers to more than 4,000 brands via sponsored content.

When new, branded content or mCent features are introduced, Jana analyzes and measures key metrics, including user attention, lifetime user value, and key performance indicators (KPIs).

As Jana and its data grew, the company's initial analytics architecture could no longer efficiently serve its business. Queries slowed and table scans became unfeasible. Adding capacity and backup systems and administering its open-sourced data repository required more and more administration time.

As illustrated in the following figure, Jana upgraded most of its data platform components to streamline its system with a cloud-based data warehouse to overcome these barriers and gain the following benefits:

- Keep pace with the business demands of processing and analyzing a rapidly growing stream of disparate data.

- Encourage an increased use of analytics throughout the company; 80 percent of Jana's employees access the data warehouse.

- Significantly reduce administration overhead.

Jana's transformation to a faster, cheaper and more effective data warehouse.

Technology Musts for Any Modern Data Warehouse

Technology innovations can improve data warehousing and analytics with regard to availability, simplicity, cost, and performance. In this section, we focus on the key technologies that should be part of any modern data warehouse.

Cloud

The properties of cloud make it particularly well-suited for data warehousing. We've mentioned these in other contexts but it's also important to know that they came from cloud:

>> **Unlimited resources:** Cloud infrastructure delivers near-unlimited resources, on demand, and within minutes or seconds. Organizations pay only for what they use, making it possible to dynamically support any scale of users and workloads without compromising performance.

>> **Save money, focus on data:** Companies that choose a cloud-built solution avoid the costly, up-front investment of hardware, software, and other infrastructure, and the costs of maintaining, updating, and securing an on-premises system. They instead focus on analyzing data.

>> **Natural integration point:** By some estimates, as much as 80 percent of data you want to analyze comes from applications outside your company's data center. Bringing that data together in the cloud is dramatically easier and cheaper than building an internal data center.

Columnar storage, processing

As mentioned earlier, columnar storage significantly improves the efficiency and performance of data storage, retrieval, and analysis, enabling quicker access to results for system users.

Solid state drives (SSDs)

Unlike hard disk drives (HDDs), SSDs store data on flash memory chips, which accelerate data storage, retrieval, and analysis. These improvements augment the computing power of data warehouses architected to use SSDs effectively.

noSQL

noSQL, short for *not only structured query language (SQL)*, describes a technology that enables storing and analyzing newer forms of data, such as data generated from machines and from social media, to enrich and expand an organization's data analytics. Traditional data warehouses don't accommodate these data types very well. Therefore, newer systems have emerged in recent years to handle these "semi-structured" data forms such as JSON, Avro, and XML.

Some of these noSQL systems were designed with the intent to replace traditional data warehouses but only ended up complementing them. To get value from this semi-structured data, organizations often have to extract and transform data from a noSQL system and load it into a traditional data warehouse for easy access by business users. As a result, this adds another layer of complexity, and cost, for companies (such as Jana; see the earlier sidebar) that attempt to capitalize on the benefits of both types of systems.

Therefore, the modern cloud-based data warehouse must incorporate, and optimize for, the ingestion and query of both semi-structured and structured (traditional) data formats so organizations avoid paying for and managing two systems.

Chapter **3**

The Criteria for Selecting a Modern Data Warehouse

The trends discussed in Chapter 2 have led to a need and an opportunity for a new kind of data warehouse. One built for the volume, diversity, and velocity of today's data, and for the new ways organizations use their data. Such a solution must take advantage of key technology innovations, including the cloud.

When you're in the market for a data warehouse, a checklist of criteria will help determine which alternative best meets your needs. Consider this chapter your checklist for finding the best data warehouse solution for your organization.

Meets Current and Future Needs

True elasticity has its business benefits but there's more to that story. You should be able to scale both compute and storage independently so you are not forced to add more storage when you really just need more compute, and vice versa. These are key capabilities of an elastic data warehouse.

Accommodates and Integrates All Data in One Place

Non-traditional, or semi-structured data, as discussed in previous chapters, can enrich the insight of data analytics beyond the limits of traditional data. But this requires a new approach to loading and transforming these new data types before an organization can analyze that data. Most traditional data warehouses sacrifice performance or flexibility to handle these data types. A modern data warehouse should eliminate the need to design and model rigid, traditional structures upfront that would require transforming semi-structured data before loading. It should also optimize query performance against semi-structured data while still in its native form. Overall, the data warehouse should support diverse data with flexibility and avoid performance issues.

Efficiently loading all of your data into one location is crucial. But integrating all of those diverse data types for more precise analytics is something else. A modern data warehouse should automatically integrate your semi-structured data, once confined to noSQL systems, with structured data inherent to a traditional, corporate relational database. There should be nothing to install and configure, with tuning and performance built in. Most importantly, you shouldn't have to maintain and pay for two separate systems to manage all of your data.

Supports Existing Skills, Tools, and Expertise

Traditional data warehouses are only outdated because the technology spans four decades and is not easily re-engineered for the cloud. That also means the language they rely on, SQL, remains an industry mainstay. Because of this, there is a broad array of mature and emerging data management, data transformation, integration, visualization, business intelligence, and analytics tools that communicate with a SQL data warehouse. The well-established role of standard SQL also means a huge number of people have SQL skills.

Traditional data warehouses support SQL but don't support the capabilities needed to effectively store and process semi-structured data. Many organizations have therefore turned to alternative approaches, such as noSQL solutions. The limitations of these systems pose another problem. They require specialized

ANALYZING DISPARATE DATA AT CHIME

Chime (chimecard.com) is smarter banking for the mobile generation. Chime gathers and analyzes data across mobile, web, and back-end server platforms to enhance its members' experiences while delivering value to its business.

Analyzing key business metrics at Chime were laborious and involved gathering and analyzing data from a large number of services, including Facebook and Google ad services. Chime also pulled events from other, third-party analytics tools, most of which provided semi-structured data such as JSON.

Chime satisfied the following requirements with its new, cloud data warehouse:

- Efficiently deliver structured and semi-structured data, and make it available for query in near real time using standard SQL database tables.

- Simplify its data pipeline without the need to design a new model for every new data type loaded into its data warehouse.

- Scale up and down to meet workload demands and control costs.

- Integrate quickly and painlessly with third-party, data analytics tools.

- Enable SQL instead of other options that require complicated programming languages to extract and analyze data.

Chime's analysts now model more scenarios to enhance member services, spend less time waiting on query results, and spend more time analyzing data.

knowledge and skills that aren't broadly available and may not support SQL. A modern data warehouse should be architected with leading technology but built on inclusive and established standards (such as SQL) compatible with skills and tools commonly available in the industry.

When you're in the market for a new data warehouse solution, consider the skills and expertise required to manage and use the solution. Hiring people with hard-to-find skills and retraining others throughout your organization to deploy and maintain a data warehouse can cost time and money.

TIP

Saves Your Organization Money

A conventional data warehouse can cost millions of dollars in: licensing fees, hardware, and services; the time and expertise required to set up, manage, deploy, and tune the warehouse; and the costs to secure and back up data. In addition, building a data warehouse that meets the business requirements and takes full advantage of the volume and variety of today's data is often cost prohibitive for any organization.

A modern data warehouse should meet these challenges at a much lower price point. For example, does it scale storage and compute separately so you only pay for the resources you need? Does it also scale workloads and concurrency? Will it support diverse data structures and integrate diverse data in one place? And finally, can it do all of this automatically without the complexity, expense, and headache of manually tweaking and tuning the system to get the best performance? (See Chapter 5 for comparing cloud data warehouses.)

REMEMBER

With cloud data warehousing, your service fee should cover everything for a small fraction of the cost of a conventional, on-premises solution. But not all cloud-based solutions are the same. Their differences also determine how much a customer must pay, in one way or another, to gain valuable data insight.

Provides Data Resiliency and Recovery

Many types of data warehouse failures can cause data loss or inconsistencies. Therefore, your data warehouse must keep your data safe, up to date, and available. Traditional data warehouses typically protect data by performing periodic backups, which consume valuable compute resources and interfere with ongoing workloads. Periodic backups also require additional storage and often fail to include the most recent data, resulting in data inconsistencies.

A modern data warehouse should manage itself when it comes to ensuring the durability, resiliency, and availability of the system. It shouldn't interfere with any ongoing workloads, degrade performance, or result in service unavailability due to backup processes running in the background. And it should be cheap, with clever ways to preserve your data without having to copy and move it somewhere else.

Secures Data at Rest and in Transit

Data security covers the following two main areas:

>> **Confidentiality:** Preventing unauthorized access to data

>> **Integrity:** Ensuring the data isn't modified or corrupted

A modern data warehouse must also support multilevel, *role-based access control* (RBAC). This insures users only have access to data they are permitted to see. For better security, require *multi-factor authentication* (MFA). With MFA, as a user logs in, the system sends a secondary verification request, often to a mobile phone. The passcode sent to the phone must then be entered. This insures that an unauthorized person with a stolen username and password cannot access the system

Encrypting the data, which means applying an encryption algorithm to translate the clear text into cipher text, is another required security feature. A bigger part of the solution is "key management." Once you encrypt your data, you'll use an encryption key to decrypt. In addition to data, you have to protect the key that decodes your data (see Figure 3-1). How long do you use the same key? What happens if the key is compromised? All of this must be managed. The data warehouse should use a hierarchical key wrapping approach, which encrypts the encryption keys, as well as a robust key-rotation process, which limits the time any single key is used.

Illustration provided by Snowflake.

FIGURE 3-1: How to protect the keys that decode your data.

In addition, the solution provider of a modern cloud data warehouse must perform periodic security testing, known as *penetration testing*, to proactively check for vulnerabilities. The vendor must administer these measures consistently and automatically without impacting performance.

Choose a data warehouse with industry standard, end-to-end security. Find a solution that has passed security audits like SOC 2.

Streamlining the data pipeline

The *data pipeline* refers primarily to the *extract, transform,* and *load* (ETL) processes that import data into the warehouse and in a format that supports queries. A slow data pipeline forces users, such as analysts, to spend too much time waiting to access data. The rapid growth in diversity, number, and volume of non-relational data sources streaming in from multiple sources compounds the problem.

A modern data warehouse should reduce the overall complexity of the process to move data through the data pipeline faster. Modern solutions should be able to efficiently load semi-structured data in its native format and make it immediately available for query without needing additional and intricate systems, such as noSQL, to transform data. This allows users to immediately access data in the same way they query a SQL database. Such solutions can provide access to new data exponentially faster, reducing the ingestion and transformation process from a day to less than an hour.

Optimizes Your Time to Value

Deploying a solution should not be a major undertaking, and crucial aspects that were once manual should be automated. Most of all, the solution you choose should be available all the time to all users, and encompass all data types at a fraction of the cost of traditional systems. Such a system should deliver immediate data insight to help streamline an organization and increase its ability to serve customers and lead its industry.

Every data warehouse solution requires time to implement. However, some solutions take considerably more time than others. Think about how long your company will need to wait before it can start to capitalize on the new system.

Chapter **4**

On-Premises versus Cloud Data Warehousing

When you're in the market for a new data warehouse, the first choice to consider is where you want your data warehouse located: your organization's data center or in the cloud and provided as software-as-a-service. Traditional on-premises data warehousing is a mature, well-established technology designed well before cloud became a viable platform. With the rapid adoption of cloud, there's a need for data warehouse solutions that can take full advantage of what the cloud offers.

In this chapter, we present the key considerations for cloud data warehousing as we compare it to traditional, on-premises systems.

Evaluating Time to Value

Deploying a conventional data warehouse (see Chapter 3) can take at least a year and extend to a multi-year project before you extract insight from your data. The agility of business today means key stakeholders who support the project, and key business and technical enablers responsible for the project's success, may leave the team or the company before going live. Such a long cycle also exposes the project to economic downturns, company revenue shortfalls, and the risk of never implementing the project due to scope creep.

In addition, on-premises solutions aren't geared to handle today's semi-structured data. That requires adding an open-source, noSQL platform, which adds another layer of complexity. This added burden lengthens the implementation phase of a new data warehouse.

Done right, a cloud data warehouse can be up and running in less than six months, or even in three months. Therefore, most of the time required to get up and running should be extracting data from your other data sources and configuring a front-end, analytics tool to extract insight from the data warehouse.

Accounting for Storage and Computing Costs

On-premises data warehouses are expensive in terms of hardware, software, and administration:

>> **Hardware:** When estimating hardware costs, consider the costs of servers, additional storage devices, data center space to house the hardware, a high-speed network to access the data, and the power and redundant power supplies needed to keep the system up and running. If your warehouse is mission critical, add the costs to configure a disaster recovery site.

>> **Software (licensing):** Organizations frequently pay hundreds of thousands of dollars in software licensing fees for data warehouse software and add-on packages. Additional end users, including customers and suppliers, who are given access to the data warehouse, can significantly increase those costs. Then add the ongoing cost for annual support contracts, which often comprise 20 percent of the original license cost.

>> **Administration:** An on-premises data warehouse needs specialized, *information technology* (IT) personnel to deploy and maintain the system. This creates a potential bottleneck when issues arise and keeps responsibility for the system with the customer, not the vendor.

A cloud data warehouse replaces the upfront and ongoing cost of an on-premises system, with simple usage-based pricing. You pay a monthly fee based on how much storage and computing resources you use. Conservatively speaking, the annualized cost for a cloud data warehouse solution can be one-tenth of a similar, on-premises system.

Sizing, Balancing, and Tuning

For optimum performance, an on-premises data warehouse must be sized, balanced, and tuned, which requires a significant upfront investment along with ongoing monitoring and administration costs. Such a configuration often includes:

>> Number and speed of central processing units (CPUs)

>> Amount of memory

>> Number and size of disks for required storage capacity

>> Input/output (I/O) *bandwidth* (a measure of how much data can be transferred at a given time)

With an on-premises data warehouse, companies often size their system for peak usage, which may represent only a small period of the year. For example, a company may need the full power of the data warehouse only at the end of each financial quarter or year. But they must pay for that peak capacity 24 hours a day because the system can't easily scale up or down.

Elastic cloud data warehousing delivers two key advantages:

>> The complexities and cost of capacity planning and administration — sizing, balancing, and tuning the system — should be built into the system, automated, and covered by the cost of your subscription.

>> The same goes for dynamically provisioning storage and compute resources on the fly to meet the demands of your changing workloads in peak and steady usage periods. Capacity is whatever you need whenever you need it.

Considering Data Preparation and ETL Costs

An on-premises data warehouse must extract data from all of your data sources. Then it must transform that data to adhere to the often rigid data structure inside the system *before* loading it into the warehouse. A key challenge includes adhering to a finite and expensive amount of processing capacity and storage. As a result, data transformation must happen outside normal business hours to avoid competing with other data processing jobs. This is expensive. In addition, semi-structured data doesn't arrive in neatly organized and consistent rows and columns inherent to traditional data structures. The data is also high-volume, high-velocity data.

The best cloud-based solutions can load semi-structured data directly without transforming it. These solutions can provide access to fresh data up to fifty times faster than a traditional data warehouse. In addition, the lower cost of unlimited, cloud storage provides data analysts access to all of the data instead of being limited to periodic aggregates of that data.

Adding the Cost of Specialized Business Analytic Tools

As mentioned in Chapter 3, traditional, on-premises data warehouses aren't geared to handle the volume, variety, and velocity of today's data. As a result, organizations operate two data platforms: an on-premises, enterprise SQL data warehouse for storage of traditional relational data, and a noSQL big data platform, which can run on-premises or in the cloud, for storing non-relational data.

Unfortunately, these newer systems require specialized tools and expertise, which don't compare to the prevalence of SQL tools and expertise. After all, SQL has been around for decades, while noSQL systems are relative newcomers.

The ideal cloud data warehousing solution delivers the best of both worlds — the flexibility to integrate relational and non-relational data along with support for the readily available SQL tools and skills for querying that data.

OPTIMIZING DOUBLEDOWN'S DATA PIPELINE

CASE STUDY

DoubleDown, an online gaming studio, added a noSQL system to their data pipeline to prepare data for loading into their data warehouse. But this approach meant DoubleDown's daily event log (user clicks and other data generated by gamers' activities) required long processing times. The company couldn't access the previous day's data until 3pm the next day. Even worse, if one of its data computing clusters went down, the company actually lost data.

DoubleDown chose a system that could directly load its semi-structured data without transforming it first, making that data immediately available for queries. This improved the quality and performance of their data pipeline by:

- Getting data to analysts nearly 100 times faster — 15 minutes versus 24 hours.

- Eliminating nearly all of the frequent failures in their previous pipeline.

- Providing analysts full data granularity instead of periodic aggregates.

- Reducing DoubleDown's cost of their data pipeline by 80 percent.

DoubleDown analysts now have immediate access to data from new product releases to enable the business to make far faster, data-driven decisions.

TIP

When you're in the market for a new data warehouse, consider the cost and availability of the skills and expertise required to manage the data warehouse, and the many analytics and other tools used in conjunction with a data warehouse.

Making Allowances for Scaling and Elasticity

Conventional data warehouses are prone to system slowdowns and crashes as users and processes compete for limited resources. These systems tightly connect storage and compute onto a single computer *cluster* (a group of computers), making it costly to increase one without increasing the other.

Newer, cloud-built data warehouse solutions provide virtually unlimited storage and compute; however, consider a data warehouse that scales storage separate from compute (see Figure 4-1). Ideally, the cloud data warehouse should scale in three ways:

>> **Storage:** Cloud storage is inherently scalable, easily adjusting the amount of storage to meet changing needs.

>> **Compute:** The resources used for processing data loads and queries should easily scale up or down, at any time, as the number and intensity of the workloads change.

>> **Users and workloads (concurrency):** Solutions with fixed computing resources slow as users and workloads increase. Organizations are often forced to replicate data into separate data marts, shift some workloads outside of normal business hours, and queue users to preserve performance. Only the cloud can enable a data warehouse to "scale out" by distributing virtual data warehouses, or clones, of the data across separate compute clusters.

TIP

Look for a cloud data warehousing solution that decouples storage from compute so both can scale easily and independent of each other to keep costs low. The solution should also scale out, or horizontally, to support more users and workloads without negatively impacting performance.

Scaling and Elasticity

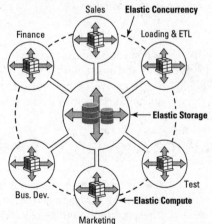

Illustration provided by Snowflake.

FIGURE 4-1: The ideal data warehouse should scale in three ways.

Deliberating Over Delays and Downtime

Many companies with on-premises solutions have two main complaints. They must wait hours or more than a day before data collected the previous day is in the warehouse and available. They must wait the same time for a complex query to run on a large data set. In some cases, multiple, concurrent processes can freeze or crash the system, extending delays and downtime.

With virtually unlimited storage and compute resources, cloud data warehouse solutions, architected as dynamically elastic, are better equipped to scale up, and out, to meet increased demands. However, decreasing delays and eliminating unplanned downtime requires more than simply ramping up system resources. Better solutions streamline the data pipeline and store data to make queries run more efficiently without manual tuning.

As you evaluate your options, look for solutions that address all these types of performance issues. How quickly you can access your data and analytics can significantly impact your operations and your ability to maintain a competitive edge.

Considering the Costs of Security and Potential Security Breaches

A single breach can quickly turn into a public relations nightmare and result in lost business, and steep fines from regulatory agencies. Although the cloud attracts the fear of security risks, it can be more secure than your data center.

If you opt for an on-premises data warehouse, you're solely responsible for securing sensitive data, which involves careful and constant attention to the following details:

>> Firewall protection

>> Security protocols

>> Data encryption, at rest and in transit

>> User roles and privileges

>> Monitoring and adapting to emerging security threats

Effective data security is complex and costly to implement, especially in terms of human resources. Poorly implemented security measures expose you to even more costs if breached.

Because cloud data warehousing providers serve a number of customers, they can afford the expertise and resources to provide industrial-strength, end-to-end data warehouse security. Look for a provider that ensures industry-standard, end-to-end encryption to secure data both at rest and in transit.

Paying a Premium for Data Protection and Recovery

On-premises data warehouses are vulnerable to data loss from equipment failure, power outages or surges, theft or vandalism, and disasters (fire, flood, earthquake, and so on). To protect your data, you must back it up regularly and store backups at a remote location. A backup power supply is also necessary to prevent data loss and ensure that your data warehouse is always available to process incoming data and queries. If disaster does strike, you'll need skilled personnel in place to recover data using the most recent backups. If your data warehouse is mission critical, you may also need a geographically separated disaster recovery site (an additional data center) along with the software, licenses, and processes to insure automatic failover so there is no gap in service.

The cloud provides an ideal solution for data protection and recovery. By its nature, it stores data off premises. Some, but certainly not all, cloud-based solutions automatically back up data to two or more separate physical locations. If the data centers are geographically isolated, then they also provide built-in disaster recovery. Cloud data centers are equipped with redundant power supplies so they remain up and running even during lengthy power outages. Cloud data warehousing providers can deliver these protections at a much lower cost than you by distributing the cost over thousands of clients.

TIP

If you do not want to administer your own data backups be sure to ask your potential cloud data warehouse provider how they configure their service. Likewise, if you need disaster recovery protection, be sure to confirm the provider's architecture uses geographically separated centers.

Chapter **5**

Comparing Cloud Data Warehouse Solutions

The growing adoption of cloud has caused legacy on-premises vendors and recent market entrants to offer cloud versions of their data warehouse products. Like any product or service, no two cloud data warehouse solutions are the same. In this chapter, we explain some of the differences and what to look for among cloud data warehouse solutions.

Understanding Approaches to Data Warehousing in the Cloud

Technology vendors all provide access to a data warehouse deployment via the Internet and typically operate on a subscription or usage-based model. But the following cloud approaches offer significantly different product capabilities:

» **Infrastructure-as-a-service (IaaS):** This approach requires the customer to install traditional data warehouse software on computers provided by the cloud platform provider. The customer manages all aspects of the cloud hardware and data warehouse software. In addition, the capabilities of the data warehouse are identical to the same software deployed using on-premises hardware.

>> **Platform-as-a-service (PaaS):** With this hybrid approach, the data warehouse vendor provides the hardware and software as a cloud service. The vendor manages the hardware deployment, software installation, and software configuration. However, the customer manages, tunes, and optimizes the data warehouse software.

>> **Software-as-a-service (SaaS):** With the SaaS approach, the data warehouse vendor provides all hardware and software as part of its service, including all aspects of managing the hardware and software. Typically included in the service are software and hardware upgrades, security, availability, data protection, and optimization.

With all of these scenarios, the task of purchasing, deploying, and configuring the data center space, and the hardware to support the data warehouse, transfers from the customer to vendor. Beyond that advantage, the benefits and drawbacks of the different offerings can vary from ease of use to security and availability. This chapter discusses some of the key differences among various cloud data warehouse offerings.

REMEMBER

If a data warehouse provider merely supplies access to its traditional data warehouse via the cloud, the solution is likely to resemble its original, on-premises architecture and funtionality.

Comparing Architectures

Many vendors offer a cloud data warehouse originally designed and deployed for on-premises environments. These traditional architectures were created long before the cloud and its benefits emerged as a viable option. Alternatively, any data warehouse solution built for the cloud should capitalize on the benefits of the cloud (See Figure 5-1).

TIP

To identify a solution built on a cloud-optimized architecture, look for the following characteristics:

>> Centralized data storage

>> Independent scaling of compute and storage resources

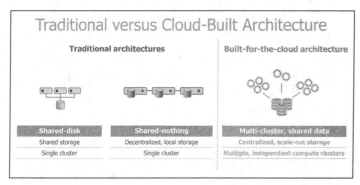

FIGURE 5-1: How a cloud-optimized architecture streamlines performance.

>> Increased concurrency without competing for resources

>> Load and query data simultaneously without degrading performance

>> A robust metadata service that applies across the entire system. (*Metadata* is data about other data such as file size, the author of the data, and when it was created.)

A cloud-optimized architecture also takes advantage of storage-as-a-service, where data storage expands and contracts automatically and transparently to the user. Data storage designed for older architectures remains expensive and has limited scalability.

Assessing a Solution's Ability to Manage Data Diversity

A key factor driving the adoption of cloud data warehousing stems from the growing volume of data that originates in the cloud – outside a company's data center. In most cases, this non-relational data must be transformed before loaded into a traditional data warehouse on-premises or in the cloud. This approach adds significant complexity and delays to accessing new data.

With this greater volume and variety of data, the cloud has become a natural integration point. An ideal way to address this issue is with a cloud data warehouse that can handle both relational and non-relational data, and without having to transform the non-relational data or compromise performance during the data loading or subsequent query process.

Data must be transformed before it's loaded into a traditional, cloud-based warehouse. Or the organization must buy and maintain an additional system to handle non-relational data.

Gauging the Scaling and Elasticity of Different Options

Not all cloud data warehouses feature the same type of elasticity. Advanced cloud data warehouse solutions can scale up and down, on the fly, and without taking the system offline or putting it into a read-only mode.

Consider the drawbacks of solutions that don't scale well:

>> A cloud data warehouse that requires manual reconfiguration involves careful planning and coordination with the vendor to scale resources.

>> Scaling may require downtime or a switch to read-only mode to redistribute data and reconfigure the system.

>> Most cloud data warehouse offerings bundle compute and storage on the same node, requiring customers to scale both when they need to increase just one or the other.

Comparing Concurrency Capabilities

Concurrency is the ability to perform two or more tasks simultaneously or allow two or more users access to a computing solution. In a traditional data warehouse, fixed compute and storage resources limit concurrency. With cloud, however, compute and storage are not fixed. Cloud-optimized architectures support concurrency in the following two ways:

>> Dynamic distribution of data and additional compute resources makes it possible for multiple users to query the same data simultaneously without degrading performance.

>> Loading and querying can happen concurrently. The cloud data warehouse solution should enable separate compute resources (nodes or even clusters) for different workloads. This approach enables simultaneous loading and querying of data without contention by assigning the conflicting processes to independent compute clusters.

Ensuring SQL Support

Almost all business intelligence (BI); extract, transform, and load (ETL); and data analytics tools can communicate with a data warehouse that supports standard SQL. However, not all cloud data warehousing solutions fully support standard SQL. For example, big data solutions positioned as "cloud data warehouses" are often noSQL solutions and have only incomplete or non-standard SQL support.

Checking Backup/Recovery Support

With on-premises and many cloud data warehousing solutions, customers must protect their own data with backup and data replication tools. However, some cloud data warehouse solutions include data protection as a part of the service.

REMEMBER

For optimum protection, look for a solution that automatically saves past versions of data or automatically duplicates data for use as an online backup. The solution should also allow for self-service recovery of lost or corrupted data.

Confirming Resiliency and Availability

Resiliency is the ability of the data warehouse to continue to function automatically in the midst of component, network, or even data center failure. *Availability* is the ability users have to access the system at all times (often referred to as "uptime"). Cloud data warehouse services vary as to how much the customer is responsible for availability and resiliency. At the most basic level, a cloud data warehouse service may require the customer to handle system monitoring to detect and possibly prevent a failure. The customer may also have to administer data replication so a duplicate copy of the data warehouse is available in case of a failure. At the other end of the spectrum, the vendor provides monitoring, replication and automatic failover as part of the service.

Availability is also a factor for software upgrades. Different vendors take different approaches during the upgrade:

>> **Basic:** Customers manage upgrades and related downtime.

>> **Better:** The vendor manages upgrades and informs users of upcoming upgrades so they can plan for the downtime.

>> **Best:** The vendor provides transparent upgrades without involving users or subjecting them to any downtime.

Look for how many 9's of availability the cloud data warehouse solution supports (99.9XX% uptime).

TIP

Gauging Performance

One of the great promises of the cloud is the ability to have huge amounts of resources available that you can pay for only when you need them. Imagine renting a Ferrari for that one important occasion but using a fuel-efficient hybrid for your everyday drive to work. Look for a cloud data warehouse solution that can optimize performance on demand and eliminates administrative effort to incorporate new resources.

Steer clear of data warehouses that disrupt or delay activity to add or subtract resources. Some solutions also require administrative work, including redistributing data and recalculating metadata such as statistics.

WARNING

Evaluating Cloud Data Security

The cloud is often perceived as less secure than on-premises data storage. However, cloud solutions have gained increasing acceptance due to the continuing barrage of break-ins into "secure", on-premises data centers. These incidents reveal that companies are limited in their ability to secure their own data.

All cloud data warehousing offerings shift the responsibility for physical data center security to the cloud solution vendor. But be aware that security features vary among vendors:

» The most basic cloud data warehouse offerings provide only security capabilities, leaving things like encryption, access control, and security monitoring to the customer.

» Other solutions offer features such as encryption and access controls, which customers can choose to turn on, but they leave the system vulnerable if not enabled.

» Cloud data warehouse offerings that are more service-orientated incorporate features for security and also assume the burden of security management by providing encryption, encryption key management, key rotation, intrusion detection, and more, as part of the service.

Accounting for Administration

Traditional data warehouses require a significant amount of the customer's time, effort, and expertise. One or more database administrators (DBAs) must perform software patches and upgrades, data partitioning and repartitioning, index management, workload management, statistics updates, security management and monitoring, backups and replication, query tuning and rewriting, and more.

At a base level, a cloud data warehouse solution that's built on older, on-premises technology still requires the customer to manage all of these aspects. Newer data warehousing offerings reduce or eliminate much of this management overhead through new designs and automation.

Ensuring the Ability to Isolate Workloads

A key factor in the speed and performance of a data warehouse is its ability to isolate workloads. Without this ability, workloads compete for the same limited resources.

With traditional on-premises systems, the only way to isolate workloads is to schedule them to run at different times. This assumes the load can finish during those off hours and also assumes no one starts a report that continues to run into the wee hours of the night. In this way, there is no contention for the CPU and memory of the system. Otherwise, the only real option is to buy additional memory or CPUs, or both.

A cloud data warehouse built on an older architecture is likely to behave the same. To be effective, the cloud data warehouse should easily configure multiple pools of compute resources (of varying sizes) to separate the workloads of users and processes that need to run concurrently. This approach eliminates contention and provides resources sized to each workload. Ideally, these separate workloads should access the same data simultaneously, and turn on and off easily, based on need.

Enabling All Use Cases: Cloning and Time Travel

In traditional environments, different data systems handle different use cases — a data warehouse for operational reporting, data marts for departmental reporting and analytics, data lakes for data exploration, and specialized tools for activities such as predictive analytics. Each of these require hardware, a copy of data, individual management, and so on.

To bring these diverse use cases together in the cloud, a data warehouse should support fast and efficient ways to clone data to avoid the traditional and costly forms of duplicating data.

A cloud data warehouse should also make it easy to recover from errors or problems created by data transformation jobs with features such as time travel, which enable simple access and rollback to previous versions of data.

Chapter **6**

Six Steps to Getting Started with Cloud Data Warehousing

Now that you know data warehousing basics, the differences between on-premises and cloud data warehousing, and the differences between various cloud data warehouses, you're probably wondering how to apply your newly acquired knowledge to choose the right cloud data warehouse for your organization.

When choosing a cloud data warehouse, you want to be sure to check off the following six steps:

- ❑ 1. Evaluate your data warehousing needs.
- ❑ 2. Migrate or start fresh.
- ❑ 3. Establish success criteria.
- ❑ 4. Evaluate cloud data warehouse solutions.
- ❑ 5. Calculate your total cost of ownership.
- ❑ 6. Set up a proof of concept (POC).

In this chapter, we guide you through these six key steps to choosing a cloud data warehouse. It starts with evaluating your data warehouse needs and ends with the process of testing your top choice. By the end of this chapter, you'll have a plan to help you choose your next solution with confidence.

Step 1: Evaluate Your Data Warehousing Needs

The data warehouse that's right for you should meet your current needs and be flexible enough to accommodate your future needs. Therefore, consider the nature of the data you work with, the skills and tools already in place, your usage needs, the future plans for your business, and how a data warehouse can take your business further than you imagined:

>> **Data:** What types of data must the data warehouse contain? At what rate is new data created? How often will data move into the warehouse? What crucial data can't you access today?

>> **Fits with existing skills, tools, and processes:** What tools need to connect to the data warehouse? What skills from your current team are applicable to the various cloud data warehousing options? What processes will a cloud data warehouse impact?

>> **Usage:** Which users and applications will access the data warehouse? What types of queries will you run? How much data will users need to access, and how quickly? How will workloads vary over time? What performance requirements do your users and applications require? Ideally, how many users should access the data warehouse but don't today due to resource constraints?

>> **Resources:** What human resources are available to manage the data warehouse? How much investment do you wish to make to monitor and manage availability, performance, and security?

Step 2: Migrate or Start Fresh

Every cloud data warehouse project should start with assessing how much of your existing environment should migrate to the new system, and what should be built new for a cloud data warehouse. These decisions may address everything from design of the extract, transform, and load (ETL) processes to data models and software development lifecycle methods. Here are a few key considerations:

>> **Is this a brand new project?** If so, it often makes sense to design the project to take full advantage of the capabilities of a cloud data warehouse rather than carry forward an implementation with significant constraints.

>> **How satisfied are users with your current implementation?** High levels of satisfaction may indicate it's best to maintain many of the existing processes and approaches from those deployments. Low levels of satisfaction/adoption indicate change is needed.

>> **What aspects of current deployments were designed to accommodate constraints that are no longer present with a cloud data warehouse?** Tools and processes designed to work around resource constraints, avoid the disruptive effort required to add capacity, or to optimize cost may be unnecessary for a cloud solution.

>> **How do current users and applications access the data warehouse?** Users and applications that primarily rely on industry standard interfaces, such as SQL, and use standard ETL and BI tools, will experience significantly less change to adapt to a new approach.

>> **How are your data and analytics requirements likely to change in the future**? A solution built to evolve is less likely to be replaced sooner than expected.

REMEMBER

If you have a large and complex traditional data warehouse environment, you may want to migrate a small part of the system to get comfortable with using a cloud data warehouse. Then you can iteratively expand your cloud footprint.

Step 3: Establish Success Criteria

How will you measure the success of moving to a new cloud data warehouse? Choose important business and technical requirements. Criteria should focus on the performance, concurrency, simplicity, and total cost of ownership.

RESOLVING LATENCY ISSUES AT WHITE OPS

White Ops is a leading provider of cyber security services. Unlike traditional approaches that employ statistical analysis, White Ops combats criminal activity by differentiating between robotic and human interaction, working to uncover and characterize new fraud patterns. This constant process requires storing and processing massive amounts of data.

White Ops had previously relied on noSQL systems to store and process that data. However, that approach required a developer to build a custom query. The latency for results was at least 24 hours, depending on the workload. The more requests, the longer the delays.

To simplify and standardize the process to increase productivity and performance, White Ops implemented a cloud data warehouse with SQL as its core language and delivered as a service. Analysts can now access data directly and without a developer. The data warehouse enables White Ops to:

- Have all data in one place
- Scale elastically
- Query diverse data with standard SQL
- Accelerate the pace of evolution of its fraud prevention offerings

White Ops can now consolidate and scale massive amounts of data, enable access to the data without waiting for specialists with deep programming skills, and help its customers avoid the potentially devastating effects of online fraud.

REMEMBER

If your new cloud data warehouse has capabilities that weren't available in your previous system, and those capabilities are relevant to evaluating the business and technical success of your new solution, be sure to include them.

As you establish the success criteria of your new solution, determine how you'll measure that success:

>> Determine which criteria are quantifiable and which are assessed qualitatively.

>> Determine how you'll measure the quantifiable criteria.

>> Figure out how you'll assess the qualitative criteria.

Step 4: Evaluate Cloud Data Warehouse Solutions

Once you determine your data warehouse needs and success criteria, you're ready to start evaluating solutions. Throughout this book we've described the differences between available options in detail (see Chapters 3, 4, and 5). As you compare solutions, make sure they meet the following criteria:

>> Addresses current and future needs

>> Integrates structured and semi-structured data, stores it all in one place, and avoids the need to create data silos

>> Supports existing skills, tools, and expertise

>> Guards against data loss and enables you to easily recover lost data

>> Secures your data with industry-standard password protection and encryption

>> Ensures data and analytics are always available

>> Streamlines the data pipeline so that new data is available for analysis in the shortest possible amount of time

>> Optimizes time to value, so you can begin to reap the benefits of your new data warehouse as soon as possible

>> Isolates workloads, so workloads do not compete for limited resources

>> Scales compute and storage independently and automatically, and scales concurrency without impacting performance

Step 5: Calculate Total Cost of Ownership

If your choice of a cloud data warehouse solution comes down to price, consider the total cost of ownership. For a conventional data warehouse, total cost of ownership includes the cost of each of the following:

>> Licensing, typically based on the number of users

>> Hardware — servers, storage devices, networking, and so on

>> Office space to house the data center

>> Electricity to run the hardware and keep it cool

>> Administration and maintenance

>> Data security — password protection and encryption

>> Ongoing management of the data warehouse

>> Solutions to ensure availability and resiliency

>> Support for scaling and concurrency

>> Creation of development and staging environments

For some solutions, you may need to consider additional costs, such as building and managing multiple data marts, having multiple copies of data in different data marts, training people, having multiple systems (for example, SQL and noSQL) to handle diverse data, and so on.

Calculating the costs of cloud data warehouse options is usually easier, but it varies according to the vendor's services. Assuming you outsource everything to the vendor by choosing a data-warehouse-as-a-service (DWaaS), you can calculate the total cost of ownership based on the monthly subscription fee. If you opt for an infrastructure-as-a-service (IaaS) or platform-as-a-service (PaaS) solution (see Chapter 5), you need to add the costs of whatever software, administration, and services the solution doesn't include.

TIP

Companies typically calculate the cost ownership over the expected lifetime of the data warehouse, which is commonly one to three years. A key caveat is that in their calculations people often assume that a cloud system runs 24/7, which is not the case. They overlook the savings possible when a cloud solution is scaled up and down dynamically in response to changing demand.

Step 6: Set Up a Proof of Concept (POC)

After investigating different cloud data warehouse options, viewing demos, asking questions, and meeting with each vendors' team, you should do a proof of concept (POC) before deciding which to choose. A POC is a process of testing a solution to determine how well it serves your needs and meets your success criteria. Think of it as a test drive. It typically lasts a day or two, but it can be conducted over the course of several weeks. You request a POC from a prospective vendor with the general understanding that if the solution performs satisfactorily, you'll buy the product. Or, in the case of cloud data warehousing, subscribe to the service.

TIP

This is also your chance to think outside the box. Consider what else you could do above and beyond what you do today. If you had this cloud data warehouse solution in place, what additional business value could this system deliver?

WARNING

When setting up your POC, list all requirements and success criteria, not just the issues you're trying to resolve. For example, if your primary complaint about your current data warehouse is that queries take too long to run, don't focus solely on that issue. Your POC should cover everything, including ease of migrating your data to the new warehouse, loading new structured and semi-structured data, running queries and multiple workloads, and using your existing business intelligence tools.

TIP

Develop a comprehensive check list. Use your list of data warehousing needs and your criteria for success as a starting point. But don't overlook positive qualities of your existing data warehouse that are non-issues for you now. In other words, make sure the new data warehouse can do everything your current data warehouse does but better, and that it overcomes the drawbacks of your current warehouse.

If you do a POC with multiple vendors, try to use the same check list for each.